The Gift of God's Name

יְהֹוָה

Christian Faith Declarations Centered Around God's Hebrew Name

Jeanne Metcalf

1st Printed by Jeanne Metcalf 2015
Revamped, Expanded, Republished 2022
2nd Printing 2022

Cegullah Publishing
International Copyright © 2022
www.cegullahpublishing.ca
All rights reserved

ISBN 978-1-926489-78-0

COPYRIGHT MATTERS

This book is an original Book written by Jeanne Metcalf and published by Cegullah Publishing. Cover and contents are copyright material, and therefore, protected by international copyright laws.

No part of this book may be reproduced, stored in a retrieval system, or transmitted in any form or by any means, electronic, mechanical, photocopied, recorded or otherwise for personal or commercial use without the prior written permission of the author. To obtain permission please contact Cegullah Publishing.
 (www.cegullahpublishing.ca)

Cover photo © istock.com
Cover design by Jeanne Metcalf.

ABOUT THESE DECLARATIONS

THE NAMES:

This Book honours the Hebrew names of our God. In the first section, it uses the name of God found in the First Covenant[1], יהוה, as seen on the cover and explains their meaning. In the second section, declarations present themselves, *primarily*, around the nine common, compound Hebrew titles of God. Additionally, declarations use the Hebrew name the angel related to Mary (Miriam) and Joseph (Yac'ov), namely, Yeshua. Use of these biblical names help believers to further their knowledge of the many titles of God from scripture, increasing their understanding about the nature and character of God, and familiarizes the reader with the Jewish name of Jesus, Yeshua. *Please note: If you are not comfortable saying the Hebrew names such as Yeshua (Jesus), or YeHoVaH Shalom, (YHVH our Peace), substitute with what suits you best.*

THE FOUNDATION:

Next, these declarations, *centered around scriptural principles*, contain faith-packed statements focusing on the benefits of the cross of Calvary, specifically, around the blood of Yeshua[2]. Additionally, these declarations include promises of the scripture to quicken our mortal

---

[1] This is the Bible's title for what many believer's call the Old Covenant.

[2] "And they **overcame** him by the blood of the Lamb, and by the word of their testimony; and they loved not their lives unto the death". Revelation 12:11 (KJV)

bodies as mentioned in the book of Romans[3]. This helps believers to increase their faith in God for health and healing in their body.

*Please note: These declarations are **not** word for word scriptural quotes from any version of scripture. Their phraseology often parallels that of the King James Version of the Bible; however, they are not direct quotes. Rather, they are capsulated biblical concepts made into easy statements, which depict principles of scripture. This promotes understanding of the Word of God to appropriate the principles first person, and thus strengthen the faith on a personal or corporate level.*

For example: under the title, YeHoVaH Yir'eh (Provider) we find these declarations:

- *Yeshua fed 5000 people with merely five loaves of bread and two fish. He knew the principles of Your Kingdom and taught them to His disciples. With Your help, by faith, I declare that I understand and utilize those principles.*
- *Thus, as a disciple of Yeshua, I recognize and acknowledge that Your Kingdom suffers no lack. I realize the power of YeHoVaH to provide in all things, even supernaturally where necessary. I look to You to provide.*
- *I believe in Your provision for me and others. You saw ahead to this day and provided all things necessary to*

---

[3] And if Christ *be* in you, the body *is* dead because of sin; but the Spirit *is* life because of righteousness. But if the Spirit of him that raised up Jesus from the dead dwell in you, he that raised up Christ from the dead shall also quicken your mortal bodies by his Spirit that dwelleth in you". Romans 8:10-11 (KJV)

the sustenance of my life and for those You placed in my care.
- *I have excellent work habits and I give my best in that area, functioning well in the position of earth wherein You placed me.*
- *I am a good steward of what You have given me, giving faithfully to the poor and the work of YeHoVaH as You lead me.*

THE PURPOSE:
These declarations are designed to help believers align their thoughts and the words of their mouth with the concepts of scripture. They offer a way of learning scriptural principles in a simple manner. Additionally, declaring these principles position believers to agree with the witnesses to truth that God gave us[4].

1 John 5: 7-8   For there are three that bear record in heaven, the Father, the Word, and the Holy Ghost: and these three are one. And there are three that bear witness in earth, **the Spirit, and the water, and the blood:** *and these three agree in one.*

THE INTENDED RESULT:
These declarations intend to further the understanding of all Christian believers, young in the faith or otherwise. To accomplish our task over a broad base of believers, we use a phraseology within the King James Version of the Bible, however, **they are not direct quotes**[5]. Their content

---

[4] Deuteronomy 19:15 (b) at the mouth of two witnesses, or at the mouth of three witnesses, shall the matter be established.

[5] To help a younger generation understand truth, these declarations are not direct quotes. Scriptural references are *not* included after each

presents the biblical principle at hand[6]. As a result, believers should come away with a simple, working knowledge of some basic Christian principles to help them walk in victory.

THE REQUIRED TIMEFRAME: 30 minutes to an hour, depending on the individual or corporate use.

> These declarations speak about many Christian beliefs, such as the blood of the Lamb, the infilling of the Holy Spirit, divine healing, walking in the dominion given to believers through the cross, as well as the believer's position seated in heavenly places.
>
> *If you embrace these faith principles*, use the approximately 4,000-word declarations in this Book to strengthen your faith, and help align yourself with what God designed for you, as a Christian believer.
>
> TIME REQUIREMENTS: Some individuals require 30 minutes to read the declaration pages, while others need an hour.
>
> *(If you wish to know more about Cegullah Publishing's approach to Christianity, please look at our faith statement at cegullahpublishing.ca.)*

---

section. However, the majority of the foundational scriptures are found in the back of the book. These declarations are designed to *highlight scriptural principles*, not word for word translations.

[6] At the time of their writing, a PowerPoint teaching on these declarations is slated for upload to cegullahpublishing.ca.

INDEX

SECTION 1: EXPLANATIONS
(Of the Names of יהוה (YeHoVaH)

	What is in A Name?	11
1.	YeHoVaH Tseva'ot (of Hosts)	15
2.	YeHoVaH Rof'ekha (My Healer)..............	17
3.	YeHoVaH Shammah (is There)................	20
4.	YeHoVaH Mekaddishkhem (My Sanctifier).	22
5.	YeHoVaH Nissi (My Banner)....................	24
6.	YeHoVaH Ro'i (My Shepherd)	27
7.	YeHoVaH Tsidkenu (My Righteousness)....	29
8.	YeHoVaH Shalom (My Peace)..................	31
9.	YeHoVaH Yir'eh (My Provider)...............	33

SECTION 2: DECLARATIONS
(With the Names of יהוה (YeHoVaH)

	Glossary of Hebraic Terms	38
	About the Blood of the Lamb Declarations	39
1.	YeHoVaH Tseva'ot (of Hosts)	41
2.	YeHoVaH Rof'ekha (My Healer).............	42
3.	YeHoVaH Shammah (is There)................	44
4.	YeHoVaH Mekaddishkhem (My Sanctifier).	45
5.	YeHoVaH Nissi (My Banner)....................	48
6.	YeHoVaH Ro'i (My Shepherd)	50
7.	YeHoVaH Tsidkenu (My Righteousness)....	52
8.	YeHoVaH Shalom (My Peace)..................	54
9.	YeHoVaH Yir'eh (My Provider)...............	56
	In Conclusion...	58
	About the Author...................................	62
	About Cegullah Publishing......................	65
	Bible Studies by This Author...................	63
	Scriptures (Declarations' Origin)...............	60

DISCLAIMER: As a publishing company, we acknowledge that we hold no power to change your life and thus, make no promise to do so. Our focus is to point our readers to God. Thus, we present these declarations as *a reminder* of God's promises.

If you, as a believer, *declare these statements in faith, looking to God to change your life through His power,* you should see amazing results, as many others have found in their life.

SECTION 1: EXPLANATIONS

Of The Names Of Yehovah

PLEASE NOTE:

This section contains only a brief amount of information about the names of God. This section presents the subject matter of the nine compound names of יהוה, to help the reader familiarize themselves with the names of God and how they can affect a believer's life, so they are understood when making the declarations within this book. It is a simple, straight to the point presentation, only.

WHAT IS IN A NAME?

Exodus 3:15 And God said moreover unto Moses, Thus shalt thou say unto the children of Israel, The LORD (יהוה) God of your fathers, the God of Abraham, the God of Isaac, and the God of Jacob, hath sent me unto you: this is my name for ever, and this is my memorial unto all generations.

God's Name is a gift to His People, given for all generations. Unfortunately, many Christian believers either overlook or do not understand the beauty of the gift of the name of God. Instead, due to tradition and other reasons, believers are told to substitute the name of יהוה with the word, LORD. In doing this, believers miss much, including some impressive blessings.

This Book invites believers to speak the name יהוה of God, which many pronounce Ya Hoe **VaH**,' accenting the last syllable[7]. In doing so, each person who says the name of God opens a door for awesome blessings as they make

---

[7]Note the pronunciation of His name varies. Nehemiah Gordan, a modern Hebrew scholar, places the accent on the last part of the name, as is common in much of the Hebrew language.

these declarations. It takes diligence, but for those who wish to put in the effort, the rewards promise to surpass the efforts.

A NAME'S IMPORTANCE:

Names are important. They help us to know one another. They relate a person's identity. However, in ancient times, names meant more than an I.D. tag. Biblical names relayed a message about a person's character, and sometimes, their destiny.

- God's first creative human, He named Adam, meaning "first man."
- Eve, who Adam named, meant "mother of all the living." This gives a clear indicator that Adam believed God's message of a coming Saviour as promised in Genesis 3:15.
- Methuselah, the longest living human named in the Bible, Enoch named. Enoch, called the people prior to the flood to repent. In warning of God's coming judgment, Enoch named Methuselah to give a message to those to whom he preached. Methuselah means, "when he is dead, it shall come." His name signified the time of a coming judgment. Additionally, as Methuselah lived 968 years, we see God's mercy actively demonstrated since God delayed His promised judgment as long as possible!

We agree that people and their individual names are both necessary and important. So is the use of their name! Likewise, the names or titles God gave us about Himself has great significance. Looking at those names, we learn more about God, His character, His nature as well as some powerful promises associated with that name, or title.

Look what Exodus promises regarding the name of God:
Exodus 20:24 "An altar of earth thou shalt make unto me, and shalt sacrifice thereon thy burnt offerings, and thy peace offerings, thy sheep, and thine oxen: in all places where I record my name, I will come unto thee, and I will bless thee."

In this verse, there are several points God stated:
- An altar of earth you shall make for Me.
- You shall sacrifice thereon the burnt offering and peace offerings, sheep, and oxen.
- In all places where I record my name, I will come unto you and I will bless you.

We know by the contents of this verse, its first two points apply only to those living under the First Covenant[8] and thus do not apply to believers in Messiah today, namely:
- The altar of earth.
- The sacrifices offered thereon.

The third point in Exodus 20:24, however, still applies, today. In fact, there are certain places where God has printed His name, and has not removed it, even in our times.
- *In Jerusalem.* God's Name is there, written in the form of the letter Shin "w" carved in the topography of the land[9].

---

[8] Hebrews 8:7 and 9:1 refer to the covenant given to Israel by Moses at the giving of the First Covenant.

[9] Many teachings on this subject are found by searching the internet. Pinterest has many articles, too numerous to list here.

- *In the heart.* A picture of the human heart shows the letter Shin "w" outlined in the structure of the heart. This shows us that God desires every person to know Him, and through redemption become the temple of His Holy Spirit[10].

We can conclude from these things, as well as a knowledge that scripture does not retract use of the name of YeHoVaH, this principle within Exodus still applies today: In other words, God wishes to bless His children, for using His First Covenant name.

As you declare the names of YeHoVaH yourself, may you experience, abundantly, the many blessings of speaking God's Covenant name as found in the First Covenant.

THE GIFT OF THE NINE COMPOUND NAMES:
God revealed certain compound names, which reveal certain aspects about God's character, all of which were seen in Yeshua as He dwelt in our midst. Before getting into use of the declaration, which in many places highlight these needed qualities in believers, let us take a quick look at these nine compound names, looking at the scripture (KJV), the main message or promise, how Yeshua's life demonstrated that aspect of God, and how believers should see it in their life.

Next, **let us understand those wonderful names!**

---

[10] On this subject, we also find information on the internet. Again, look at Pinterest.

YEHOVAH TSEVA'OT
YHVH of Hosts

יהוה צבאות

2 Samuel 6:2 "And David arose and went with all the people that [were] with him from Baale of Judah, to bring up from thence the ark of God, whose name is called by the name of the LORD of hosts that dwelleth [between] the cherubims."

MAIN MESSAGE OR PROMISE:
This name of God, YeHoVaH of Hosts, means the Lord of the armies (of heaven). This scripture presents a direct reference to the Ark of the Covenant, which held the Mercy Seat, the specific place where God promised to meet those He appointed to stand before Him, namely His High priest.

Other uses of this name shows God as the One who fought for Israel, going out before them for the purpose of giving them rest. That rest is a ceasing from struggles or battles in the flesh as one tries to order their life in full dedication unto God. Instead, through the provision of our Salvation in Messiah, we rest in Him. Through the Holy Spirit's power and presence in believers, we live before God in full dedication to Him for His plans and purposes and thus, touch the lives of those around us.

IN YESHUA'S LIFE:
Yeshua is YeHoVaH Tseva'ot. In His capacity as Redeemer, He went out before all humankind to give them rest from struggling on their own to win battles against unrighteousness (sin) in their own life. Through salvation, we have Eternal Life and a powerful release from our struggle with sin because Yeshua made it possible for us to live by His Spirit, thus ceasing from living a life of sin. Our part is to yield to the Spirit's leading.

IN THE BELIEVER'S LIFE:
When in Messiah, we enter a place of rest. From that place, we live out our life. No matter the situation, we can rest in God and trust Him. We demonstrate God's abilities to "fight for all mankind" when we enter our rest[11].

---

[11] For more about God's rest, please see the book, "Thy Kingdom Come," Entering God's Rest in Prayer. It explains this principle of rest clearly.

2

YEHOVAH ROF'EKHA
YHVH My Healer

יהוה רפאך

Exodus 15:26 "And said, If thou wilt diligently hearken to the voice of the LORD thy God, and wilt do that which is right in his sight, and wilt give ear to his commandments, and keep all his statutes, I will put none of these diseases upon thee, which I have brought upon the Egyptians: for I [am] the LORD that heals thee."

MAIN MESSAGE OR PROMISE:
In the body of this scripture, there are several points to consider:

- Diligently listen to the voice of the Lord.
- Do that which is right in His sight.
- Hear (which implies obeying) His commandments and statutes.

If, under the First Covenant, these conditions were fulfilled then, a promise was realized:

- No diseases came to Israel as upon the Egyptians. *(In other words, no curses like those of the Egyptians came to Israel as long as Israel obeyed God's commands.)*

The Exodus, with the event of Passover, shows a prophetic picture of people purchased from the slavery of sin. Once purchased, the redeemed ones are expected to live as God sees "correct," not doing what is right in their own eyes, but rather, doing what is right in God's eyes. These people purchased by God, are designed to be a people focused on obeying God's voice.

Under the New Covenant, obedience is also important. Healing comes to believers as a result of the promises of God, that which Yeshua attained by His precious blood at Calvary. Whether under the New Covenant or the Old, the message here is clear: **God is the One who heals His People**.

IN YESHUA'S LIFE:
In reading the gospels, we see many miracles, which Yeshua performed such as healing the sick and even raised the dead back to life. To touch Yeshua, in faith, meant healing of whatever ailment afflicted the body. Yeshua called Himself the "Good Shepherd" who laid down His life for His Sheep. (John 10:11). Broken lives, and every part of their being, are healed today because of the amazing gift of Yeshua.

IN THE BELIEVER'S LIFE:
Believers can learn from our Good Shepherd, showing others His compassionate care, expressing it in many different ways. We are called to obey Yeshua's command

found in Mark 16:15-18: *"And he said unto them, Go ye into all the world, and preach the gospel to every creature. He that believeth and is baptized shall be saved; but he that believeth not shall be damned. And these signs shall follow them that believe; In my name shall they cast out devils; they shall speak with new tongues; They shall take up serpents; and if they drink any deadly thing, it shall not hurt them; they shall lay hands on the sick, and they shall recover"*.

A believer's prayer life extends past their own needs to cover the needs of others, everywhere. As we exercise effective intercession on behalf of others, thinking along the line of a Shepherd, we speak God's Word into situations, and help those in need. A true believer is an active contributor to their environment, demonstrating God's character in all their dealings, including the one of a good shepherd who willingly lays down their life for others.

3

YEHOVAH SHAMMAH
YHVH is There
יהוה שמה

Ezekiel 48:35 "[It was] round about eighteen thousand [measures]: and the name of the city from [that] day [shall be], The LORD [is] there."

MAIN MESSAGE OR PROMISE:
Ezekiel saw a vision of the Lord's Temple in Jerusalem. When this temple comes to earth, the name of the city will be, The Lord is there, of YeHoVaH Shammah. While this promise is future, it shows an aspect of YeHoVaH's: He is there, which means He is where You need Him to be. In fact, there is no place one can flee from His presence[12]!

IN YESHUA'S LIFE:
When Yeshua walked the earth, YeHoVaH was there within His Temple, meaning the living, moving, and breathing body of Yeshua. When Yeshua walked anywhere, YeHoVaH was there! That presence demonstrates the principle of YeHoVaH Shammah wonderfully.

---

[12] Psalm 139:7

IN THE BELIEVER'S LIFE:

Believers, in the New Covenant, are the temple for God, on earth: *1 Corinthians 6:19 What? know ye not that your body is the temple of the Holy Spirit, which is in you, which ye have of God, and ye are not your own?* Wherever believers go, YeHoVaH is there, also! So, let each believer live his/her life reminiscent of the presence of the Lord within him or her, demonstrating, the Lord in our midst is mighty[13]!

---

[13] Zephaniah 3:17

4

YEHOVAH MEKADDISHKHEM
YHVH My Sanctifier

Exodus 31:13 "Speak thou also unto the children of Israel, saying, Truly, my sabbaths ye shall keep: for it [is] a sign between me and you throughout your generations; that [ye] may know that I [am] the LORD that doth sanctify you[14]".

MAIN MESSAGE OR PROMISE:
YeHoVaH stated that the Sabbath day is a particular day that we set apart for Him. This day is to be unlike any other day. On that day, YeHoVaH asks us to cease from our worldly labours. Looking to the *principle* of the Sabbath day, a day set apart, we see that God is set apart, too, different from all others who may call themselves a god. He also sets His people apart unto Himself for His unique purpose:

Deuteronomy 14:2 For thou art a holy people unto the LORD thy God, and the LORD hath chosen thee to be a peculiar people unto himself, above all the nations that are upon the earth.

---

[14] Please note, the words holy and sanctify are from the same root meaning: to set apart

IN YESHUA'S LIFE:

Yeshua lived His whole life set apart or sanctified unto God and for God's purposes alone. He subjected Himself to the will of His Heavenly Father, which meant obedience to earthly parents when He was young, and later meant obedience unto death, a death of crucifixion, in order to bring about our salvation.

As Yeshua walked out His life upon this earth, He lived that life in perfect righteousness, living apart from sin, the world, and all its lures. To look at Yeshua, to see His behaviour in His life is to see a person truly set apart for YeHoVaH alone. To see His passions, His miracles, and even the commission He left to His disciples, is to recognize that Yeshua demonstrated YeHoVaH as the One set apart from all others. Truly, there is none other like our God!

IN THE BELIEVER'S LIFE:

We, as believers, receive our sanctification through Yeshua and are called to live out our life apart from the world, we have a privilege of showing others that our God is different from any other being this world knows. While we are positionally sanctified or set apart for God, we should live out that separateness before the eyes of those in this world.

5

YEHOVAH NISSI
YHVH My Banner

יהוה נסי

Exodus 17:15 "And Moses built an altar, and called the name of it Yahweh Nissi"

MAIN MESSAGE OR PROMISE:
In relating the event of a battle between the children of Israel and the Amalekites, Moses, (the author of Exodus), made a specific note to record, for all of time, an altar he built to honour YeHoVaH for the victory. He named the altar, "Yahweh Nissi[15]."

During the battle, Moses positioned himself upon a hilltop. He lifted the rod of YeHoVaH above his head. Whenever he held that rod high above his head, the Israelites saw it, looked to it and believed. As they pressed onward, they prevailed over the adversary, but whenever Moses got tired of lifting his hands above his head and lowered his arms and the rod which he held, Israel began to lose the battle.

---

[15] KJV interprets it as Jehovahnissi.

Aaron, and Hur, (two important Israelite leaders), positioned themselves on the hilltop beside Moses to hold up his hands so the rod remained lifted up. In doing so, Israel won the battle. When the battle was finished, Moses, in honour of YeHoVaH Who delivered them, built an altar commemorating that miraculous victory. Truly, God gave that miracle and other victories. He is our banner[16]!

IN YESHUA'S LIFE:
Yeshua, throughout His lifetime upon the earth, conquered the spiritual adversary of humankind on every front. He never lost a battle, (sinned, fell into temptation or failed to do YeHoVaH's will). No, not even once. Yeshua is our miracle, our banner. In fact, the scriptures declare Yeshua as the ensign (banner) for all nations[17]. In looking to this ensign, we live! Yeshua indeed showed this in His life and in His death. When in need of a miracle, a victory, we look to the ensign for all nations. We look to Yeshua!

IN THE BELIEVER'S LIFE:
Every battle believers face, whether within or without, with YeHoVaH on our side, aligns us for victory. In fact, our life in Messiah was formed by YeHoVaH to be victorious in all things. At times, it might not look like a victory to us, or even to others, but we never have the total revelation of all things as we live upon the earth. We see that fact as we read this chapter in Hebrews and listen to its message:

---

[16] Moses on the hilltop with the rod above his hands depicts the cross of Yeshua. Whoever looks on Calvary and believes has victory!
[17] Isaiah 11:12

Hebrews 11: 32 And what shall I more say? for the time would fail me to tell of Gedeon, and of Barak, and of Samson, and of Jephthae; of David also, and Samuel, and of the prophets: 33 Who through faith subdued kingdoms, wrought righteousness, obtained promises, stopped the mouths of lions, 34 Quenched the violence of fire, escaped the edge of the sword, out of weakness were made strong, waxed valiant in fight, turned to flight the armies of the aliens. 35 Women received their dead raised to life again: and others were tortured, not accepting deliverance; that they might obtain a better resurrection:

36 And others had trial of cruel mockings and scourgings, yea, moreover **of bonds and imprisonment:** *37* **They were stoned, they were sawn asunder, were tempted, were slain with the sword: they wandered about in sheepskins and goatskins; being destitute, afflicted, tormented;** *38 (Of* **whom the world was not worthy:) they wandered in deserts, and in mountains, and in dens and caves of the earth.** *39 And these all, having obtained a good report through faith, received not the promise*[18]*:* *40 God having provided some better thing for us, that they without us should not be made perfect.*

Ours is the victory, but it comes in the form that God desires to give it to us. We maintain our faith and somehow, as we depend upon God and follow His plans, aligning ourselves with His Sovereign will, we demonstrate that God is our miracle. It is all tied in with Calvary. Indeed, He is our banner. He is greater than the circumstances, reigning far above it!

---

[18] Bold face not in original text

6

YEHOVAH RO'I
YHVH My Shepherd

יהוה רעי

Psalm 23:1 "The LORD [is] my shepherd; I shall not want."

MAIN MESSAGE OR PROMISE:
King David, as a young boy, shepherded for his father. He learned how to care for those sheep, including how to fight predators that desired to destroy the flock. He even risked his own life in the process of caring for those sheep. Later, when David was King of all Israel, he declared YeHoVaH to be His Shepherd. Truly, David saw YeHoVaH cared for Him, and for Israel, in a healthy and protective fashion, just as David protected his father's sheep.

Regarding YeHoVaH, He is a Shepherd over His people, caring for them in every aspect of our being. He takes care of His children every moment of every day and onward into eternity.

IN YESHUA'S LIFE:
Yeshua, when living upon the earth, watched over His Disciples, giving them instructions, and caring for them

in every way. In fact, Yeshua called Himself the "Good Shepherd" who laid down His life for His Sheep. (John 10:11).

IN THE BELIEVER'S LIFE:
As a believer, we can learn from our Good Shepherd and show others His compassionate care, expressing it to our fellow human beings in many different ways. We can also take care of the many things entrusted to us by God, for example, our prayer life, which extends past our own needs to cover the needs of others, saved and unsaved alike.

As we exercise effective intercession,[19] thinking along the line of a Shepherd, we should use the "rod" and a "staff" entrusted to believers. We do this by speaking God's Word into situations and helping those in need. It is not wisdom for a believer to be a passive participant upon this earth ,but rather, an active contributor demonstrating, in all that we do, God's character, including the one of a good shepherd who willingly lays down their life for others. That means self-less love!

---

[19] If you do not understand that principle, consider taking the course, "Molded for the Miraculous."

7

YEHOVAH TSIDKENU
YHVH My Righteousness

יהוה צדקנו

Jeremiah 23:6 "In his days Judah shall be saved, and Israel shall dwell safely: and this [is] his name whereby he shall be called, THE LORD OUR RIGHTEOUSNESS."

MAIN MESSAGE OR PROMISE:
This passage of scripture above refers to a future time in Israel. At that time, Judah will be saved, and Israel will dwell in safety. This is a clear reference to God dwelling in their midst. Total righteousness, the sign of God's rule, will be seen easily at that time.

IN YESHUA'S LIFE:
When Yeshua dwelt amongst humankind, He fully demonstrated the qualities of the Lord our righteousness. One incident of such righteousness is found in the following passage:

Luke 9: 54 And when his disciples James and John saw this, they said, Lord, wilt thou that we command fire to come down from heaven, and consume them, even as Elias did? 55 But he turned, and rebuked them, and said, Ye know not what manner of spirit ye are of.

IN THE BELIEVER'S LIFE:
Our salvation, through Yeshua, procured for us the righteousness of Yeshua. In God's eyes, we are righteous. Our lives, however, must demonstrate that righteousness as we exercise our choices throughout our life as a believer. As we do this, we demonstrate God's righteous choices to others including His choice of mercy, compassion, and a desire for all to share in Eternal Life.

8

YEHOVAH SHALOM
YHVH My Peace

יהוה שלדם

Judges 6: 24 "Then Gideon built an altar there unto the LORD and called it Jehovahshalom: unto this day it [is] yet in Ophrah of the Abiezrites."

MAIN MESSAGE OR PROMISE:
YeHoVaH appeared to Gideon. He called Gideon to be an instrument empowered by the Holy Spirit to set Israel free from their bondage to their enemies. Gideon left that encounter with YeHoVaH fearful that he would die for having such an encounter with God. After being reassured he would live, Gideon built an altar in the place of that visitation and called it Yahweh Shalom. It meant the place of peace.

IN YESHUA'S LIFE:
Yeshua came to bring peace to all humankind, but not with a sword. He did not wish to destroy men's lives but to save them! At Yeshua's first coming, it was not the day of vengeance, so He extended the gift of salvation, which

when accepted, brings a deep peace that the world can never take away.

IN THE BELIEVER'S LIFE:
Believers are to live in peace: *peace between humankind and God, and peace between humankind and humankind.* Yeshua's peace, which He gave believers, the world cannot take away. As believers live out their life from that place of peace and as they extend the message of peace to others, namely the gospel, they show God's peace to all.

John 3:17 "For God sent not his Son into the world to condemn the world; but that the world through him might be saved."

9

YEHOVAH YIR'EH
YHVH Our Provider

יהוה יראה

Genesis 22:14
"And Abraham called the name of that place Jehovahjireh: as it is said [to] this day, In the mount of the LORD it shall be seen."

MAIN MESSAGE OR PROMISE:
Abraham, in obedience to the Lord's command, placed Isaac upon an altar of sacrifice. As Abraham lifted his hand to make Isaac an offering, God called out to Abraham not to harm the child. First of all, this situation was a one-time test, which demonstrated a prophetic type of Messiah, and secondly, Abraham's actions proved that he loved God above the gift of his special child, Isaac.

Abraham then saw a ram caught in a thicket. He sacrificed that ram in Isaac's place and thus, Isaac did not need to die. Abraham's willingness to do so, prophetically showed Yeshua at Calvary. Just as God provided a ram for Isaac, which Abraham found caught in a thicket, God provided our substitute for our sin's punishment with Yeshua, our Saviour.

- This incident is a prophetic picture of Calvary.
- The message here is that God provides for everyone, a "substitute" for their sin, so they need not die eternally for their sin.

An Added Thought:
- From that point on, the Jews took the horns of a ram, hollowed it out, and used it as a form of trumpet. That trumpet is called a shofar.
- When blowing the shofar, among its many purposes, is a reminder that God is our Redeemer.

IN YESHUA'S LIFE:
Yeshua is the substitute for us regarding the problem of our sin and its associated punishment, in God's eyes. Due to Yeshua's sacrifice on Calvary, we need not die for our sins. Yeshua is our provision, first, for sin, and then, in every other way, including provision for all of our earthly needs.

When Yeshua walked the earth, the gospels tell of two occasions when He provided physical sustenance. On one occasion, He fed five thousand men plus women and children, and on another occasion, He fed four thousand men plus women and children.

Yeshua clearly demonstrated, in His Life upon the earth, the character of Yahweh Yir'eh.

IN THE BELIEVER'S LIFE:
When we think of this name, Yahweh Yir'eh, we should think of the Lord as our Provider. In Hebrew, Yir'eh literally means "the one who sees ahead." When we have

a need, God has already seen that need, and just as the ram waited in the thicket for Abraham to discover and use in his situation, our provision waits for us. We only need to trust God and ask Him to open our eyes so we may realize that provision.

Yeshua told us, "Seek ye first the kingdom of God and His righteousness and all these things shall be added unto you." Matthew 6:33. As a believer, as we go about doing the work as God assigned us to do, putting Him first in all things, we can expect to receive whatsoever we need to accomplish the task. Additionally, we can trust our God to provide for us in our daily needs for in God's Kingdom, there is no lack!

SECTION 2: DECLARATIONS

For those who are interested, the declarations contain a 3,941-word counta

GLOSSARY OF HEBRAIC TERMS

NAME	MEANING
Yeshua	Jesus
Ha' Mashiach	The Messiah or the Anointed One (Christ)
Adonai	Lord
YeHoVaH	First Covenant Name of God
Tseva'ot	Hosts
Rof'eka	Healing
Shammah	There
Mekaddishkhem	Sanctifier
Nissi	Banner
Ro'i	Shepherd
Tsidkenu	Righteousness
Shalom	Peace
Yir'eh	Provider
Ha satan	The adversary - (satan)

ABOUT THE DECLARATIONS OF THE BLOOD OF THE LAMB:

As you read these declarations, you will discover many statements which refer to the blood of Yeshua and the benefits of the cross. We include these statements as they align our words with the words of the witness of scripture.

Our Bible says,
1. Deuteronomy 19:15 b) at the mouth of two witnesses, or at the mouth of three witnesses, shall the matter be established.
2. 1 John 5:8 And there are three that bear witness in earth, the Spirit, and the water, and the blood: and these three agree in one.
3. Hebrews 12:24 And to Jesus the mediator of the new covenant, and to the blood of sprinkling, that speaks better things than [that of] Abel.

Therefore, these declarations speak of the truths about the blood of Yeshua which God desires we recognize, understand, and believe.

REGARDING THE HEBREW NAMES:

If you wish to say the Hebrew names of God, we provided a suggested pronunciation just below the writing of the name and its English meaning.

1

YeHoVaH Tseva'ot YeHoVaH of Hosts
Ya ho Vaah' Sa -va -oat

1. *YeHoVaH Tseva'ot, I agree with You for what the overcoming power of the blood of the Lamb speaks.*
2. *Yeshua purchased me through His precious blood.*
3. *Through Yeshua's precious blood, I am in the Kingdom of YeHoVaH and the Kingdom of YeHoVaH is in me.*
4. *I am a new creation. Old things passed away. All things became new. I am in Messiah and part of the one New Man.*
5. *I praise You for the resurrection power of Yeshua in my life that comes from Your Holy Spirit. I rest in that overcoming power and walk out my day in the victory of Yeshua's dominion. Therefore, I face this day knowing that with You, all things are possible.*
6. *I thank You that I dwell in the secret place of the most High, abiding under the wings of my God, YeHoVaH Tseva'ot. I say, You are my refuge and my fortress: my God in Whom I trust.*
7. *You deliver me from the snare of the fowler, and from the noisome pestilence.*
8. *You cover me with Your feathers and under Your wings I trust: Your truth is my shield and buckler.*
9. *I am not afraid of terror by night; nor the arrow that flies by day; nor for the pestilence walking in darkness; nor for the destruction at noonday.*
10. *A thousand fall at my side; ten thousand at my right hand; but nothing comes near me.*

11. Only with my eyes I see and behold the reward of the wicked.
12. I have made You my refuge, even the most High, my habitation.
13. No evil befalls me, nor any plague comes near my dwelling place.
14. You gave Your angels charge over me to keep me in all Your ways. They bear me up in their hands, so I do not dash my foot against a stone.
15. I tread upon the lion and adder: the young lion and the dragon, I trample under my feet. Your love is upon me, and I am delivered.
16. I know Your name. You set me in a high place, even in heavenly places, seated in Yeshua.
17. I call upon You, YeHoVaH, and You answer me.
18. You are with me in trouble, deliver me and honour me.
19. With long life You satisfy me and show me Your salvation.

2

YeHoVaH Rof'ekha   **YeHoVaH My Healer**
Ya ho Vaah' row-fee-kah)

1. *YeHoVaH Rof'ekha, I agree with what the blood of the Lamb speaks regarding my healing.*
2. *Through this precious blood, Yeshua paid sin's penalty and made possible all needed healing and deliverance for any oppressed by ha satan.*
3. *YeHoVaH Rof'ekha, I agree with what the Word says, You are the God, Who heals.*
4. *Yeshua bore my griefs and sorrows. He was wounded for my transgressions; bruised for my iniquities and by His stripes, I was healed.*
5. *All **hinderances,** which strive to arise against the healing that You gave through Yeshua for my life or others, I command in the name of Yeshua Ha Mashiach to fall to the ground, wither and die and bear no fruit.*
6. *I function in accordance with the benefits of the blood of Yeshua, as You designed me to function, sound in spirit, soul, and body.*
7. *All tricks, snares and traps of the adversary are exposed and removed.*
8. *I refuse to enter into agreement with fear. I choose to agree with You and walk in faith.*
9. *I recognize that Yeshua came to destroy the works of ha satan, which works included sickness, disease, infirmity. In short, all things not sourced in You.*

10. As I am in Yeshua and Yeshua is in me, in Yeshua's name I destroy the works of ha satan everywhere I go. I set captives free.
11. By Your Spirit's power, I lay hands on the sick and they recover. The blind see; the lame leap for joy; the silent speak; all in need receive healing and deliverance from Your Hand. The dead hear Your voice and live.
12. When Yeshua died, I died. When He was buried, I was buried. When He arose, I arose to new life.
13. I, therefore, live in resurrected power, seated in Yeshua in heavenly places, living the life God foreordained for me in Yeshua.
14. Through the resurrection power of Yeshua, I walk out this day in Your strength, power, might and triumph.
15. I walk in the resurrected life Yeshua attained for me.
16. I remember I am more than a conqueror through Yeshua, my Adonai.

3

YeHoVaH Shammah　　　　　　YeHoVaH is There
Ya ho Vaah' Sha-mah'

1. YeHoVaH Shammah, I praise You for the overcoming power of the blood of the Lamb.
2. Thanks to Yeshua's precious blood, I am in the beloved with You as my Father.
3. Everywhere I go Your Presence is with me. You never leave me nor forsake me.
4. You are the ever, over-flowing, ever present One. You fill me with Your Holy Spirit; therefore, I declare that I am filled with the Holy Spirit and walk in Holy Spirit power.
5. You go out before me. You stand as my rear guard.
6. I daily put on Yeshua and therefore, wear my spiritual armour.
7. I dedicate my heart to embrace Your truth, my lips to speak that truth, and my life to become a lamp to show the love of Yeshua to all I meet.
8. I remember, no matter the circumstances, situations, or surroundings, I am never alone for You are with me.
9. All You designed for me to complete, yes, every assignment You gave me to do throughout my lifetime, by the power of Your Holy Spirit, I complete.
10. I fulfill my life with You at the helm of my life and walking by my side. As I succeed, I glory only in the cross and in Yeshua Ha' Mashiach crucified.
11. By Your Spirit, to Whom I yield, I am lead into all truth.
12. Due to the discerning power of the Holy Spirit to which I yield, I walk before Your face, living my life in righteousness.

13. *I follow only Your voice and the voice of a stranger I will not follow.*
14. Due to Yeshua's overcoming power of the blood of the Lamb, I am set free from the Law of Sin and Death.
15. I live by the Law of the Spirit of Life in Yeshua, my Adonai.
16. I know how to walk in love and resurrection power for the glory of God.
17. With Your Spirit's wisdom, power, and resources, I walk out my life in You, resting in Your accomplished victory through Yeshua, wielding well the shield of faith.
18. YeHoVaH, You are my shield of faith.
19. With Your help, I recognize and defeat all thoughts, words, or accusations from ha satan, those fiery darts sent against me.
20. Every fiery dart falls to the ground and touches me not. Each one withers and dies and bears no fruit.
21. Regarding every human source involved in those fiery darts, I declare forgiveness and I speak life over their life, returning good for evil.

4

YeHoVaH Mekaddishkhem   **YeHoVaH My Sanctifier**
Ya ho Vaah' Ma-ked-dish-khem'

1. YeHoVaH Mekaddishkhem, I praise You for the overcoming power of the blood of the Lamb.
2. Through that precious blood of Yeshua, I am sanctified and sprinkled clean.
3. As a believer empowered by the Holy Spirit, I live my life not subject to the Law of Sin and Death. I live my life, with Your Help, by the Law of the Spirit of Life in Messiah, set apart, living for You alone.
4. By the Holy Spirit's direction and help, I walk in resurrection power. I do so in every situation to glorify Your name.
5. I understand the leading of the Spirit of Dominion and follow that leading, walking in all Your ways, including victory. With Your strength, power and might, I forge ahead, expanding the Kingdom of God on the earth for Your glory, honour, and praise.
6. I recognize that Yeshua, through His precious blood and the victory of the cross, defeated ha satan.
7. All the defences of the adversary fall before me, due to Yeshua's precious blood through which I overcome.
8. Therefore, I cancel all assignments of ha satan against me this day in Yeshua's name.
9. Yeshua went about doing good and healing all those oppressed by ha satan. By Him, in Him and through Him, I do the same.

10. The gospel of truth is upon my lips. You work with me setting captives free; thus, signs and wonders follow.
11. I, therefore, thank You that I am filled with the Holy Spirit and power. As I yield to Your Spirit's truth, which includes correction, my character changes day by day to look more like You. This is a good thing which I desire. No good thing do You withhold from those who walk uprightly. Therefore, as I yield to Your Spirit, Your character is seen in me.
12. I walk away from the lusts of the flesh, the lust of the eyes, the pride of life and all that is in the world.
13. I follow Your lead into all righteousness and holiness. I rest in Your ability to fill me with the Holy Spirit, flow through me and express Your Divine Nature.
14. Wherever I go, the Kingdom of YeHoVaH affects all and the will of YeHoVaH is done.

5

YeHoVaH Nissi   **YeHoVaH My Banner**[20]
Ya ho Vaah' Niss-ee'

1. *YeHoVaH Nissi, I praise You for the overcoming power of the blood of the Lamb. Due to the overcoming power of the blood of Yeshua I receive my miracle, my victory.*
2. *I declare with You living in me and walking with me, I am victorious in all situations, walking in love for all humankind.*
3. *I desire for others what I desire for myself: the victory! Therefore, I declare when praying for myself or others, just as nothing withstood Joshua taking ground for the Kingdom of God, nothing stands before me.*
4. *As Samuel declared Your Word and not one word fell to the ground, so I declare Your word and not one word spoken in the Spirit's power falls to the ground.*
5. *All strongholds, all the power of the adversary which I encounter, I overcome in Your Name and in Your strength.*
6. *This overcoming ability applies to all tactics of the adversary, seen or unseen, recognized or unrecognized and it always happens, no matter the circumstances, nor those involved.*
7. *In faith, no matter what I encounter, I step up to the challenge before me. I know that I succeed because You are with me, faithful to Your promises in and through Yeshua. I win because You are at my side.*

---

[20] Some believe it means, "miracle," due to the event linked with the naming of the altar. Exodus 17:15

8. As Israel looked to the rod of Moses as he stood on the hilltop overlooking the battle and believed for their victory, I believe YeHoVaH Nissi for mine and for those for whom I pray.
9. You cause me always to triumph in Messiah and make apparent the sweet aroma of His knowledge by me in every place.
10. I thank You that I am crucified with Messiah: nevertheless, I live; yet not I, but Messiah lives in me: and the life which I now live in the flesh, I live by the faith of the Son of YeHoVaH Who loved me and gave Himself for me.
11. I glory only in the cross of Yeshua, through Whom the world is crucified unto me, and I unto the world. I bring You glory, praise and honour, always.

6

YeHoVaH Ro'i   **YeHoVaH My Shepherd**
Ya ho Vaah' row-ee'

1. YeHoVaH Ro'i, I praise You for the overcoming power of the blood of the Lamb, which purchased me as Your own.
2. As one of Your sheep, I have Your watchful eye caring for me and so I lack nothing.
3. As my Shepherd, You lead me by still waters, and You restore my soul.
4. Even though I walk through the valley of the shadow of death, I fear no evil for Your rod and staff comfort me.
5. I praise You for Yeshua, the Good Shepherd, Who laid down His life for all humankind.
6. As He protects the sheep, which includes me, all wolves that come to draw believers away from You receive a blow of defeat.
7. I am protected by You, YeHoVaH Ro'i. I follow Your Spirit and do Your bidding.
8. Blessed be the God and Father of our Yeshua, Who has blessed us with all spiritual blessings in heavenly places in Messiah.
9. I praise You that You raised me up to sit with Yeshua in heavenly places.
10. I rest in Your total authority in all things, and I express that authority as guided by Your Holy Spirit, grateful that You positioned me in Yeshua.
11. From that place of victory, I walk out my day advancing Your Kingdom as You lead and guide me.

12. YeHoVaH Ro'i, You watch over me. You give me wisdom and insight as I watch and pray this day, so that I do not fall into temptation.
13. As a part of Messiah's Body on earth, I recognize that I am accepted in the Beloved.
14. I declare that I am not a lone soldier but recognize the need to assemble with other believers to build up and encourage each other in the most holy faith. I assemble with like-minded believers.
15. I function in my assigned position within the Body of Messiah and walk it out in faith by the resurrection power, which comes from the Spirit of Dominion, Who is Your Holy Spirit.
16. I rest in YeHoVaH's order established in the home and in the Body of Messiah.
17. YeHoVaH, with Your Help, I watch over the doors of my lips, aligning my words with Your Word and Your will for this day.
18. I am more than a conqueror, through Yeshua Ha' Mashiach, my Adonai.

7

YeHoVaH Tsidkenu   YeHoVaH My Righteousness
Ya ho Vaah' sid-kha-new

1. *YeHoVaH Tsidkenu, I praise You for the overcoming power of the blood of the Lamb. That precious blood on the mercy seat makes me righteous in Your sight.*
2. *Yeshua paid a high price for the righteousness I enjoy in Him.*
3. *I rejoice that righteousness came to me freely as You established me in Yeshua's righteousness. No one earns that righteousness.*
4. *Even all my righteous behaviour or deeds seen by humankind and by You, I know comes from the works of the cross of Calvary. I have no reason to boast! I glory only in the cross!*
5. *Every day, as I remember Your righteous gift to me, I exalt Your Name, YeHoVaH Tsidkenu.*
6. *I rejoice that the Kingdom of YeHoVaH is not meat and drink but is righteousness, peace, and joy in the Holy Spirit.*
7. *Additionally, I put on the garment of praise for the spirit of heaviness.*
8. *All schemes, tricks, snares, and words of ha satan which come to rob me of my joy, to leave me gloomy, saddened, or downtrodden falls to the ground. Oppression is far from me.*
9. *I thank You for what is mine in Yeshua, including all blessings in Heavenly places.*
10. *I know that through Yeshua, and through His righteousness, He aligned me to walk in resurrection*

power, in the place of victory, walking in dominion as You created me to walk.
11. I choose to agree with the works of the cross of Calvary and of all that the blood of Yeshua speaks.
12. I choose to walk out my life in faith knowing that I am the head and not the tail. I am above and not beneath, in all things.
13. I am blessed in Yeshua, and I live out my life justified, sanctified, and glorified according to Your Word.
14. From my position in Messiah, through His total authority, power, and dominion, and with His name that is above all names, I command all things in my day to come into complete alignment with the will of YeHoVaH and it happens because of the dunamis power of the Holy Spirit.

8

YeHoVaH Shalom   **YeHoVaH My Peace**
Ya ho Vaah' Sha-loam'

1. YeHoVaH Shalom, I praise You for the overcoming power of the blood of the Lamb, which aligned me to receive perfect peace.
2. I rejoice that Yeshua made peace through the blood of His cross and reconciled all things both in earth and in heaven.
3. Yeshua's precious blood brought Your forgiveness in my life and a peace that surpasses all understanding.
4. It is a peace that the world cannot take away. I embrace that peace and remember that any attempt to thwart that peace is a battle.
5. I give You that battle for all battles belong to You. I rest in Your peace. I rejoice that the God of Peace bruises ha satan under my feet, shortly. I rest in Your victory and take my peace.
6. As You have forgiven me, I express Your forgiveness to others, walking in Your peace as I do so.
7. All God-ordained relationships in my life operate without brokenness but with forgiveness, expressing YeHoVaH's love.
8. As You go out before me this day, YeHoVaH, I express that perfect peace that comes through Yeshua to others.
9. I, therefore, follow You and bring the gospel of peace with me, expressing it in thought, words, and deeds through the power of the Holy Spirit.
10. I believe You have the keys to every door. As guidance for me, some doors You open, while others You close. I recognize

Your will in all situations and therefore every door You open, I walk through and every door You close, I do not enter.
11. I rest in Your Peace all this day, knowing that You keep me in perfect peace for my mind is fixed upon You.
12. I rejoice in Yeshua for He overcame the world. In Him, I overcome also.
13. I let the peace of God rule my heart. I do not fret or worry. I rest in all things, always, trusting Your ability and power to resolve situations and bring about victory.
14. I keep my mind stayed upon You and thus, I am kept in perfect peace.

9

YeHoVaH Yir'eh   YeHoVaH My Provider
Ya ho Vaah' Yir-ay'

1. YeHoVaH Yir'eh, I praise You for all provisions obtained for me through the overcoming power of the blood of the Lamb.
2. I was lost in sin, unable to rise above the power of ha satan, but through Your redemption and the power of the Spirit, I am set free, no longer a slave to sin or fear.
3. Through that precious blood I thank You that as Your child, You provide all my needs, spirit, soul and body.
4. There is no avenue, no place in my life where lack rules. YeHoVaH Yir'eh, You rule!
5. YeHoVaH Yir'eh, nothing surprises You. Neither inflation, costs of living challenges, reduced or fractured incomes, affect Your ability to provide.
6. Whatever problems of provision affecting humankind, Your Kingdom knows no lack.
7. Yeshua fed 5000 people with merely five loaves of bread and two fish. He knew the principles of Your Kingdom and taught them to His disciples.
8. With Your help, by faith, I declare that I understand and utilize those principles.
9. Thus, as a disciple of Yeshua, I recognize and acknowledge that Your Kingdom suffers no lack.
10. I realize the power of YeHoVaH to provide in all things, even supernaturally where necessary. I look to You to provide.
11. I believe in Your ability to provide for me and others. You saw ahead to this day and provided all things necessary to

the sustenance of my life and for those You placed in my care.
12. I have excellent work habits and I give my best in that area, functioning well in the position of earth wherein You placed me.
13. I am a good steward of what You have given me, giving faithfully to the poor and the work of YeHoVaH as You lead me.
14. I recognize Your provision, including resurrection power of Yeshua to help me walk as an overcomer.
15. I seek first the Kingdom of YeHoVaH, and Your Righteousness and all necessities of life are added unto me.

IN CONCLUSION

1. As I have aligned my words with Your Words, in faith I rest assured that, with Your help, I recognize and overcome every tactic which tries to keep any aspect of the victories of the cross from manifesting in my life.
2. I recognize every battle I face belongs to You. I give You that battle knowing that it is already fought and won. I accept and walk in the victory, resting my faith in Your ability to do the impossible.
3. Since you live in me and are with me, I am equipped to defeat every tactic of the adversary in my life or that of another for whom I pray. All it takes is my willingness to step up to the challenge.
4. I confess my willingness to step up to the challenge, and with Your help, I do so, expecting victory.
5. I follow Your lead in these matters and therefore, anything that tries to hold me or another in bondage, at any time or in any place, I recognize as defeated.
6. With Your help, I see the victory won and the adversary and his plans totally defeated.
7. I declare that with Your help, my heart embraces and my lips align with the witness of Scripture.
8. I speak the same thing as the Spirit, the Water, and the Blood.
9. I declare Your works and live for You, Your plans and purposes and all You desire for me, completing the works Your foreordained for my life.
10. I declare with my lips, one more time, that I live the crucified life, and trust that, by the Holy Spirit's power, it becomes a reality in my life.

11. I confess my desire and willingness to live a holy life before Your Face. I acknowledge to follow Your call to that holiness and trust Your ability to keep me in that place of holiness before Your Face.
12. With Your help, I die to self and will live free from the world's pulls, traps, snares, and influences.
13. As I lay down my life to serve You and others, I rejoice that with Your Holy Spirit's help, my service to You becomes a pleasing sacrifice to You.
14. I lean upon You in all things and refuse to take glory to myself for that which You have done in and through me. It is not by human might, nor power these things are done, but by Your Spirit!
15. I conclude these declarations by saying, one more time, my life belongs to You. My life is a place to show Yourself strong.
16. Father, may You be glorified in my day today and may the name of Yeshua be high and lifted up!

Come, Your kingdom come.
Be done Your will, be done!
As it is done in heaven above,
be it done upon the earth below.
AMEN!

SCRIPTURES
(Declarations' Origin)

These 106 scriptures are a partial base from which the declarations in this book originate.

(Not listed in order of use)

1 Corinthians 15:50
1 John 1:7
1 John 2:16
1 John 2:29
1 John 3:8
1 John 4:15
1 John 4:18
1 John 5:20
1 John 5:5
1 John 5:6
1 John 5:8
1 Peter 1:19
1 Peter 2:17
1 Peter 2:24
1 Peter 3:15
1 Samuel 17:47
1 Samuel 3:19
1 Thessalonians 2:13
2 Corinthians 12:12
2 Corinthians 2:14
2 Corinthians 2:5
2 Corinthians 5:17
2 Corinthians 5:18
2 Corinthians 5:21
2 Timothy 1:7
2 Timothy 3:16

Colossians 1:14
Colossians 1:20
Colossians 3:15
Deuteronomy 19:15
Deuteronomy 28:13
Ephesians 1:17
Ephesians 1:3
Ephesians 1:6
Ephesians 2:10
Ephesians 2:13
Ephesians 2:6
Ephesians 4:13
Ephesians 4:14
Ephesians 5:18
Ephesians 6:14
Ephesians 6:16
Exodus 15:26
Galatians 1:16
Galatians 2:20
Galatians 6:14
Hebrews 12:24
Hebrews 12:28
Hebrews 13:12
Hebrews 13:5
Hebrews 13:6
Hebrews 2:14
Hebrews 9:12
Hebrews 9:14
Hebrews 9:20
Isaiah 26:3
Isaiah 61:3
John 1:3

John 10:27
John 14:27
John 16:33
John 18:37
Luke 10:9
Luke 14:18
Luke 17:21
Luke 6:45
Luke 8:1
Luke 9:2
Mark 13:13
Mark 16:20
Matthew 12:34
Matthew 19:26
Matthew 26:41
Matthew 28:18-20
Matthew 6:33
Matthew 6:44
Philippians 2:12
Philippians 2:19
Philippians 3:9
Psalm 23
Psalm 41:1
Psalm 84:11
Psalm 91
Psalm 92:4
Revelation 1:5
Revelation 12:1
Revelation 3:7
Romans 1:17
Romans 10:10
Romans 10:4
Romans 14:17
Romans 16:20
Romans 3:22-24,26
Romans 3:25

Romans 4:22
Romans 4:3
Romans 5:21
Romans 5:9
Romans 6:18
Romans 6:3
Romans 8:1
Romans 8:14
Romans 8:15
Romans 8:2
Romans 8:37
Titus 2:14
Titus 3:5
Zechariah 4:6

ABOUT THE AUTHOR

Jeanne believes the Word of God opens a door to every person to know their God. That knowledge, once gleaned and retained, makes strong believers, who know how to stand in the real world in which we live.

Rev. Jeanne Metcalf

With these convictions in mind, Jeanne, inspired and led by the Holy Spirit, began to write in the 1990's. Soon she developed inductive[21] style Bible Studies and self-published them for her students to use. With her major goal to equip the saints, she soon discovered that her sound teachings, presented with clarity and simplicity, made an impact. As long as her listeners put in their valuable time to study scripture, and took Jeanne's advice to call upon the Holy Spirit to help them, they became powerful believers, transformed, prepared and ready to stand in their generation.

Today, past students who studied the Bible with Jeanne, as well current new students, testify to Jeanne's writing and teaching gift. They love the clarity and simplicity of the Word as she presents it in a refreshing straightforward format. Thus, they encouraged Jeanne to make her books more widely available. Therefore, Jeanne began Cegullah Publishing as an avenue to present her books to all who wish to be strong in the Lord and the strength of His might. A greater availability opens doors for more people to know their God and do exploits!

"But the people that know their God shall be strong and do exploits." (Daniel 11:32

---

[21] In the inductive Bible Study method, believers learn first by reading and studying the Word on their own, then they glean from the textbook. This study method often gives a better foundation to a believer's faith than sitting through lectures or speaker related teachings.

BIBLE STUDIES AND OTHER BOOKS
BY THIS AUTHOR as of 2022

Jeanne, up to this date in time, writes Bible Studies prayer books and devotionals. Bible Studies come with a textbook and workbook. Devotionals come as a journal, giving room for you to write your personal comments. **Note: books below are a Bible Study unless marked other wise.**

An Arsenal of Powerful Prayers [22]
  Scriptural Prayers to Move Mountains (Prayer book)
Arising Incense
  A Believer's Priesthood
Candidate for A Miracle
  Wisdom from the Miracles of Yeshua
Foundations of Revival
  Biblical Evidence for Revival
His Reflection
  What God longs to see in His People
Heaven's Greater Government
  Behind the Scenes of Earth's Events
In The Name of Yehovah We Set Up Our Banners
  Biblical use of banners
It's All About Heaven
  As Pictured in Scripture
Kingdom Keys for Kingdom Kids
  Walking in Kingdom Power
Molded for the Miraculous
  Why God made You
Releasing the Impossible
  The Limitless Power of Intercession
Salvation Depicted in a Meal [23]

---

[22] *This is a book of written prayers of assorted topics to help believers live a stronger, active faith. No workbook.*
[23] *Haggadah (Guide) for a Christian Passover. No Workbook.*

The Gift of God's Name
Christian Faith Declarations Centered Around God's Hebrew Name
The Jeremiah Generation
   God's Response to Injustice
The Warrior Bride-
   God's Kingdom Advancing through Spiritual Warfare
Thy Kingdom Come
   Entering God's Rest in Prayer
Watching, Waiting & Warning
   Obeying Yeshua's Command to Watch & Pray
   Comes with 1 textbook, 1 workbook, 1 prayer book.
When Nations Rumble
   A Study of the Book of Amos
Worship in Spirit and In Truth [24]
   The Tabernacle of David - Past, Present & Future

---

[24] *Good sister book to "In the Name of YeHoVaH we set up our banners."*

ABOUT CEGULLAH PUBLISHING

"Publishing the treasures of modern-day scribes"

Cegullah Publishing produces written materials. Since the contents is based on the Word of God, we consider our products treasures. Through these available treasures, we give opportunities for our reading audience to explore pertinent topics which steady, reaffirm, and help our readers to walk out their Christian life in victory.

CONTACT INFORMATION

For more terrific books, notebook, booklets, free downloads or to contact Jeanne, go to
www.cegullahpublishing.ca

To order a book with spiral cover, go to cegullahpublishing.ca and follow the link. To order from Amazon (perfect bound), enter ASIN# 1926489780.

www.ingramcontent.com/pod-product-compliance
Lightning Source LLC
Chambersburg PA
CBHW061249040426
42444CB00010B/2315